Enjoy!

James Hanna

Dogs I've Known

Dogs I've Known
James Milton Hanna
Copyright 2008
All rights reserved.
No part of this publication may be reproduced or transmitted in any form or means without written permission of the publisher
ISBN 1-93005243X
Library of Congress Number 2008923572

Library of Congress Cataloging in Publication Data.
Hanna, James Milton
Dogs I have known
Hunting dogs, sled dogs, watch dogs and family pets

Other books by author

Cornbread and Beans for Breakfast
A Possum in Every Pot
Beyond Yonder Ridge
The Labrador Saga
A Man Called Shiloh
Southern Tales
Once Upon a Time in the South
Milton's Guide to Self-Publishing and Marketing
Tales from Delaware Bay
More Tales from Delaware Bay
Meandering Around Delaware Bay
Musings from the Bay

Cherokee Books
24 Meadow Ridge Pkwy
Dover, DE 19904

Dedication/Acknowledgment

to

Donna Chappell for editing this book

Nora Howell for illustrations

A-Rat for the cover and other illustrations

The memories of the dogs I have known,
both good and bad

Foreword

To everyone who has ever loved a dog, owned one or wanted to own one. This book is for you. It will make you laugh and cry.

Often I think of the many dogs I have owned. Some were very intelligent, some dumb, some vicious, some lazy while others were bundles of energy. Each of my dogs reminded me of people I have known. Each had a different personality.

When it seems the entire world is against you, your faithful dog stays your friend no matter how you treat him or her. Your dogs do not see your bad side and stay true companions. There can be no truer friend than the noble beast known as dog.

James Milton Hanna
2008

Table of Contents

Dogs I've Known 7
Red 17
The Bad Dog 34
"Bud" 37
The Red Dog 63

Dogs I've Known

Dogs have been man's best friends for centuries. Kids growing up in rural areas as well as many growing up in densely populated areas have grown up with dogs in households.

Dogs fit into about every aspect of life. There is the family dog that thinks it is a part of the family and entitled to the same privileges as other members of the family. Guard dogs who respond only to commands from their master and hunting dogs who enjoy the great outdoors as much as their masters. Then there are the pitiful abandoned dogs who run wild, perhaps hoping for a master or family to which they can belong. Many dog shelters house strays and because of limited funds are forced after a period of time to put such unfortunate dogs that aren't adopted to sleep. It sounds cruel, but what else can they do?

I have been fortunate to have owned, (it is more an acceptance of each other… man and dog), a good number of dogs in my lifetime. First, there was the childhood dog, then Sled dogs that worked for their livelihood, and various other dogs over the span of many years. Each dog possessed a unique personality. I've owned dumb dogs as well as very intelligent creatures.

Describing dogs is like comparing people, the good and bad, the intelligent and the dumb. Dogs all fit in one of these characteristics.

A dog who I named Jigs was the first dog that I owned at age 10. He was a small brown and white mutt, being a mixture of who knows what. Some knowledgeable friends said that he was part Rat Terrier. My teen years were spent roaming the hills and exploring along the shores of creeks and the banks of the Tennessee River in Northwest Alabama. It was a wonderful time of innocence with a clear line drawn between right and wrong. I roamed the hills, river bottom land and along the shore of numerous rivers and streams. Jigs was my constant companion.

My earliest memory of Jigs was that of an almost grown dog that struggled between being a pup and a grown dog. He still enjoyed chewing anything he could find that was chewable. We quickly learned not to leave anything chewable on the porch or other areas where he had access.

I can't remember if he was given to me or was a stray that happened to decide to be a part of the family. Most people, in those days of so long ago, seldom kept dogs in the house. My dog Jigs was an outdoor dog. He lived under the edge of the house or porch in inclement weather. Otherwise, he would sleep under a tree or on the open porch.

Like many dogs, he couldn't resist chasing passing cars or mule drawn wagons. He once was kicked by a mule and was sick for a few days. He was a fast learner and after that incident he was careful not to get too near a mule's hoofs when chasing a passing wagon. Cars were a special hazard for Jigs. It was just something about the turning wheels of a passing car that he couldn't resist. It was an urge that he had to satisfy,—like someone addicted to drugs. Several times he attempted to bite a tire from a passing car and was flung to the side of the road. After a time he learned to avoid being hit and somehow survived to a ripe old age for a dog.

Jigs loved to hunt and chase wild animals. He and I would spend hours in the woodland hunting squirrels and rabbits. He possessed the ability to scent squirrels and because of his ability to alert me to the nearness of wild game, I often was able to shoot squirrels that Jigs treed in Hickory Nut groves and take them home for dinner. It those days of the early 1940s, when times were hard, most people ate squirrel, rabbit, quail and young groundhogs. Many people fished and fish fries became an important part of our social life. Fish fries were the equivalent of today's backyard barbecue.

One incident I will never forget was the time on a cold November afternoon immediately after school, that Jigs and I were exploring the far side of my grandfather's small farm. Over the years farmers had picked up stones from the field and piled them in one area until the pile became about ten feet around and four feet high. Over the years trees had grown up between the rocks, leaving open spaces under the rocks. In the summer the pile of rocks were what we called "snaky" and because of the danger from being bitten by a rattlesnake or copperhead we steered clear of rock piles. However, on this particular cold day there was no danger of snakes.

JIGS

Jigs started sniffing around the rock pile and became increasingly excited. Finally he started barking and chasing something that was in the rock pile. Apparently, the trees growing up through the pile of stones had created tunnels within the rock accumulation. Jigs chased whatever was inside the rock pile around and around the pile. After about four or five times of the animal being chased around inside the pile of rocks, and a frustrated Jigs being unable to get through the rocks to the animal, I started removing stones. As Jigs chased the animal toward me, I reached inside the tunnel and grabbed the creature by its tail and dragged it from the rock pile.

Perhaps it was a stupid thing to have done, but in life I have done many stupid things. The animal started struggling and suddenly I realized what I had dragged from the rock pile. It was a large skunk. At about the time it dawned on me what I was holding by the tail, the creature sprayed me in the face and I quickly let go. Jigs grabbed the skunk and also receive a blast in the face.

Then the skunk leisurely crawled back into its hole. Jigs and I had a bad problem. I rushed home as fast as I could. I was half-blind and sick all over, and of course, the odor from being sprayed by a skunk didn't help.

My mother must have smelled me coming because she came out on the back porch just as I arrived home. "What have you been up to?" she asked. She was terribly angry and told me to go to the woodshed and take off all of my clothes and bury them in the loose dirt near the shed.

Remember, it was November and cold. My mom dragged an old wash tub into the shed and started filling it with water. We didn't have indoor plumbing so most of the water was cold. She had taken water that was heating on the wood stove and mixed it with cold water. That took some of the chill off. But, it was still very cold. She emptied several mason fruit jars of tomatoes and scrubbed my entire body with the tomatoes and a bar of homemade lye soap. I was getting colder by the minute and after the scrubbing, she wrapped me in a large quilt and took me into the warm house.

Several squirrel hunters offered up to $25 for Jigs because of his ability to locate that evasive critter. That was a princely sum in the early forties, especially for a young teenager. Selling Jigs was unthinkable. He was as close to me as a brother could be. We understood each other and worked well as a team. All I had to do was point and say "sic him" and he would charge any animal I pointed out, regardless of the animal's size.

In the summer he would walk ahead of me on trails and cow paths through thick underbrush and on several occasions he would discover snakes next to or on the trail ahead of us. He would grab the snake and shake it to death. He probably prevented me from being bitten by a snake several times.

Sometimes he would attack much larger dogs and have the daylights beaten out of him. His worse adversary was a bulldog who grabbed him by the throat and almost choked him to death. It required the effort of two of us to separate the two dogs. For a couple of days after that incident he moped around home.

Jigs went with me on my first camping trip in the woods on the far edge of my Grandfather's farm. It was a crisp autumn evening when we walked the quarter of a mile across the field to the edge of a wood-lot. I selected to sleep under an oak tree that had spreading limbs and was easily climbable. I raked oak leaves into a large pile next to the tree trunk and was soon asleep wrapped in an old quilt. Jigs curled up next to me.

Sometime during the night I heard a noise of something big tramping through the crunchy frosty leaves and nearing where we were sleeping. Jigs had alerted me to the approaching creature by his deep growling. I reached over and touched the dog and found that his hair was standing up like the bristles on a brush.

All at once Jigs leaped to his feet and dashed toward the unknown creature that was approaching through the dry leaves. My heart skipped a beat as I leaped to my feet and set a record climbing the oak tree. I wondered what type of creature was approaching, was it a bear or a Mountain lion? I had never heard of one of those creatures living in Alabama in recent years. Perhaps they lived in the mountains and now they were after a meal, which was me. A young boy's imagination can run wild at such times.

As I sat on a tree limb with a rapid beating heart pondering the situation, I heard Jigs barking and chasing something toward me. I quickly climbed higher into the tree as Jigs chased the creature under and past my tree. As the creature ran under my tree, it gave out a loud "MOO, MOO". It was only a stray cow! After a short time Jigs returned and made himself a bed on my quilt. I decided that I would sleep on a limb in the tree, well above the ground. I doubted that I had the strength to climb down after being scared so badly. I didn't sleep too well, but Jigs slept quiet well and in comfort on my quilt.

When dawn finally broke, I was awakened by the sounds of the community near where I lived coming to life. First, dogs started barking, doors slamming, the sounds of cars starting and then cattle mooing and hogs squealing and grunting as they anticipated farmers coming to feed them. I climbed down from the tree and petted my faithful dog and got him to chasing his tail, which was a game, we often played. I would grab his tail and pull on the end and place it in his mouth. There after, he would chase his tail round and round until he tired of the game.

I walked ten minutes back to where I lived with my grandparents and enjoyed a delicious breakfast of hot biscuits, liberally spread with fresh butter and homemade wild grape jelly. Along with the biscuits was a platter of fried eggs and country ham. Breakfast was a serious meal for my grandfather because he worked hard on the farm and depended on a large breakfast to last him until dinner (lunch).

I forgot about Jigs and only later in the day wondered where he was. I didn't think too much about the dog for the rest of the day because I was busy doing chores. That evening I became concerned regarding his whereabouts. Maybe he had gone hunting or was visiting a dog friend somewhere?

After breakfast the next morning Jigs still hadn't come home. I became very concerned and walked back to where I had spent the night in the oak tree during my first camping trip. Jigs stood under the tree guarding the quilt that I had forgotten and left behind. I gave him a big hug and lots of belly scratching and head petting. He really enjoyed being made over. He walked back home with me with his tail wagging indicating that he was happy. He was starved and ate a larger meal than normal and couldn't seem to get enough water.

After that incident, my Grandfather and I had to be very careful about leaving anything behind in the field. If we didn't call Jigs to follow us home he would stay and guard whatever we had left in the field. Another time he spent two days guarding a plow in the backfield where my Grandfather had unhooked it from the mule team. After a time, we always made a point of calling him home with us.

The memory of Jigs, a truly boyhood companion, will always be with me. Perhaps I remember that little dog with a guilty conscience. I enlisted in the Air Force at age 17 and left the area. I was embarrassed to admit that I forgot about my faithful companion. He lasted about a year past my departure and everyday he would walk out to the general store where he and I often visited and sit and look up and down the highway longingly. One day he walked out in front of a car and was killed instantly.

Witnesses stated that after I left home he wandered around like in deep thought and seemed to have deliberately walked onto the highway in the path of an approaching car. The driver of the car was very upset about running over Jigs. But, really, it wasn't the man's fault that Jigs was killed. His death was caused by my lack of concern in leaving him. If there is a "Dog Heaven" I'm sure that the faithful companion of my youth with be there.

Red

Red was a beautiful Husky with bright red fur with white stocking feet and belly. He was about the prettiest animal I had ever seen. I was in the Military and stationed at Goose Bay, Labrador in Northeastern Canada. I had read about the Arctic during all of my early teen years and felt at home living in a land of deep snow with frozen lakes and streams. Enjoying such extreme climatic conditions might seem strange for someone who had grown up in the Deep South. It goes to show that what you read can affect your life.

I arrived at the USAF base at Goose Bay, Labrador in February 1950 and spend three years living an exciting outdoor life. I worked as a military scout in the summer and taught Arctic Survival to aircraft crews during the cold snowy months. Most people might not have enjoyed such an assignment, but to me, it was heaven. I could hunt and fish to my heart's delight. Hunting and fishing was something that I had been doing all my life since age ten.

My first dog team, (that was the only way to travel in the winter when away from the roads on base,) consisted of three dogs given to me by members of the Base's Rescue Squadron. They maintained several dog teams to assist with

Red

rescuing survivors from plane crashes. Back in those days plane crashes were more frequent. One of the three dogs was a pretty little tan Siberian Husky. She was a very gentle little dog, almost too small for pulling a sled. She was intelligent and that seemed to make up for her small size.

Not too long after I acquired her she gave birth to one small pup. Because of his beautiful color I named him "Red." This dog grew up being my constant companion. At first, I allowed him to be a part of the team without really having any expectations that he would be intelligent enough to become a lead dog.

By the time he was a year old he was pulling his share of load. After an almost disastrous experience traveling several miles across an expansion of glare ice near open water, I decided to let Red try out for the lead position. Many of the older dogs were envious and attempted to bite the rear of Red as he led the team. Occasionally, he would turn and slash one of the agitators until they were finally content to follow him as a leader.

Red made an excellent leader and showed his intelligence in many ways. On a number of occasions when traveling on trails leading through a deep forest and when the trail branched off in two directions, Red would look back at me and all I had to do was to point the trail I wanted him to lead the team. He would then take the indicated trail.

During the summer months, I served as a military scout patrolling the perimeter of the Air Base. Red was often with me and would always warn me when someone was near. He never barked like most dogs. He would growl, stop and look toward where someone was approaching.

Bob

Sometimes when we were away from the base at noontime, he would hear the base's siren that sounded at noon seven days a week. He would look toward the base and howl a few times. Many times I was so far from the base that I couldn't even hear the siren, but he could.

Unfortunately, Red contracted distemper, (a disease fatal to large numbers of dogs in the arctic,) and died at age eighteen months. That was a sad time for a person who was accustomed to having such a good companion and friend when driving the dog sled or walking patrol along the lonely outreaches of the base. Two dogs from my team died from the outbreak plus dozens of dogs throughout the area. The native dogs were not given shots and easily succumbed to such diseases as distemper and rabies.

After Red's death, I tried different dogs to lead the team of dogs pulling the sled. None of the dogs did very well as leader. A good leader must be intelligent, obedient and willing to lead and obey commands such as turn right, turn left, stop and go.

Red had fathered one pup by a Husky. She was intelligent. I had tried her as a leader but she wasn't an effective leader. I named her pup, Bob. He was large, well built and proved to be very intelligent. He resembled his father in size. Instead of the beautiful red coat, white belly and white stocking feet, he was black with white feet and belly. Still, he was a beautiful dog.

Bob not only became a good leader, but also a friend. Most of the dogs in the team loved a good fight. At the least opportunity, members of the team would slash at each other. Bob very seldom resorted to picking a fight. But once in a fight, he became a snarling demon.

Soon Bob became the dominant dog in the team and I made him the leader. At first we had some misunderstandings, like the time he led the team onto bad ice. The section of ice narrowed to about four feet wide and in deep water. It had warmed up to about twenty degrees that day. The team, led by Bob, rushed toward shore on the narrow section of ice that was breaking behind the sled. Fortunately, the dogs were able to rush ashore and pulled the sled ashore. Looking back from the direction we had traveled, I could hardly believe that we had traveled on such a narrow section of ice. Bob seemed to learn from that situation and afterwards wouldn't lead the team onto bad ice. After a time he became almost as good a lead dog as Red had been.

Once a person works with dogs, he or she starts to realize that dogs have many characteristics similar to humans. I've had lazy dogs that didn't do their share of pulling, as well as dogs that gave all their effort in pulling the sled. And then, there were trouble-makers like found in all walks of life.

My team's primary trouble-maker was a black and white spotted medium size dog. I named him "Bawls" because he was always bawling about something. His favorite trick was to nip a dog passing near him and then retreat and watch the fight that he initiated. The dog that was bitten would always lash out at the nearest dog to him. I imagine the other dogs must have developed a hatred for the mischievous "Bawls."

One day the entire team exacted their revenge on the luckless dog. It happened this way; I hitched up the team and traveled to the Hudson's Bay Company, about five miles away, to purchase a hundred-pound bag of cornmeal. In those day prepared dog food wasn't available to purchase. The dog food had to be cooked once a day using cornmeal, grease and chopped up rabbits or other available meat. It was an ordeal to have to cook the dog food each day. However, it was a necessary ordeal. The cooking of the evening dog food was very difficult when traveling on a long trip.

When I hooked the team back to the sled in preparation for returning to the remote cabin where I lived, "Bawls" did his usual thing and nipped one of the team members and as one the entire dog team turned on "Bawls."

Breaking up the fight was very difficult and resulted in me receiving several slashes on my hands and arms when I grabbed dogs by their collars and pulled them apart. After a time I managed to separate each dog. "Bawls" had a reason to bawl this time. All he could do was whimper. His entire body had cuts and rips spread about two-inches apart. I disconnected him from the team and tied him on the sled for the return trip. It was several weeks before he healed sufficiently to help pull the sled. I had to tie him directly in front of the sled so that I could protect him from the rest of the team. He was cured of nipping other team members after that. Otherwise, he did pull his load like a good dog should.

One unusual addition to my dog team was that of a dog I purchased from Indians camped about four miles away across the mile wide Hamilton River. A local native told me that the Indians who were camped in the area had a dog for sale. (In those days Indians living in Labrador still lived in tents year round) I hooked up four dogs and set out for the Indian camp. I really needed more dogs.

The Indian camp was set back in the woods amid tall black spruce trees near where a small stream flowed into the river. It was February and the ground was covered with about four feet of snow. The snow was crusted from the temperature warming to above freezing and then dropping down to about ten degrees. My team made good time.

I crossed the river to the Indian encampment and tied my team to a tree. By that time the dogs in the village were howling and my dogs were answering their invitation to a big brawl. Most of the sled dogs enjoyed a big fight with other dogs. Sometimes dogs would be killed or badly injured. Imagine being on the trail several miles from home in a wilderness area and your dog team would start a brawl resulting in several getting injured. That would result in a serious situation. Whenever the dogs would fight, the dog team driver (Musher) must quickly separate the fighting dogs.

I walked down the trail about one hundred yards to where the Indian tents were scattered through the woods. There were perhaps ten large gray tents that once were white but had turned gray from wood smoke and the elements. Indian families and relatives usually camped together.

Four Indian men walked out to meet me and one asked what I wanted. I told them that I heard they had a dog for sell. Only one of the men could speak some English and indicated that he did have a dog for sale. I asked him how much he wanted for the dog. His answer was one word, "Whiskey."

I replied, "No whiskey because it is illegal for me to give or sell alcoholic beverages to natives. I don't want the Royal Canadian Mounted Police after me."

He gave me a knowing smile.

The day before I had purchased four cartons of Camel cigarettes from the Base Exchange for $1.10 a carton and had the cigarettes tucked away inside my large parka. I offered the men two cartons for the dog. I received a resounding NO to my offer. Then I upped the offer to three cartons.

The men walked off a short distance and talked for a minute or two. They returned to where I was standing and replied that it was a deal. While one man went for the dog, I handed the other men the three cartons of cigarettes that I had offered, and then gave them the fourth carton that I had in my parka. That seemed to please them.

The man soon returned with a large black and white dog weighing about eighty pounds. The dog was snarling and leaping toward me. The Indian was restraining the dog with a leather leash. I suddenly had second thoughts about owning such a savage dog. I asked that the dog be fitted with the extra harness I had with me in the event I was able to buy the dog.

They quickly fitted the harness on the struggling dog and hooked him to the sled.

My four dogs didn't like the new dog and turned on him. He proceeded to give all four dogs a beating. The only thing that saved them from being badly mauled was the fact that the new dog was tied next to the front of the sled and couldn't reach the other dogs once they quit fighting with him.

All this time the Indians thought everything was humorous and seemed to have a smirk on their faces. I loosened the slip-knot holding the sled to a tree and the dogs lurched forward at a record pace with the new dog behind them attempting to nip their behinds if they dared slow down. Instead of returning up the frozen river to my cabin, I decided to take a long way home and tire out the new dog. I was thinking, "How am I going to unhitch this snarling demon that I have just purchased?" He had already slashed the back of my hands when I was attempting to stop the dogs fighting.

I followed the base roads in a round about way to reach the cabin that was my Scout headquarters. It was four times as far to my cabin by traveling the roads than it was to have gone up the river directly to the cabin. Never had my team raced so fast as that day with the new dog hitched to the sled behind the rest of the team. Any dog that slowed down received a nip in the butt.

When the team raced through the small Base Housing area, a large Collie was observed walking alongside the road. The team, as one, accelerated their pace in an attempt to reach the hapless Collie. The Collie realized that the team rushing toward him wasn't doing so with the intent of playing, but rather with malice.

The Collie raced from the road and across the snow filled yard for the protection of its home. The team left the road and raced through the deep snow toward the Collie. I finally turned the sled over to halt the team. The Collie's master saw what was happening, he opened the door and allowed the dog to escape back into the house.

Dog teams seem to have an instinct to chase anything running from them. There are recorded incidents of people when seeing sled dogs approaching, run to get out of the way of the team and being mauled by the dogs. The best thing to do was take a few steps to the side of the trail and the team would race past.

I reached my cabin without incident and then faced the problem of unhitching the new dog and placing a collar around his thick neck, so he could be chained.

I tied the sled to a tree and unhitched all the other dogs. I then approached the Indian dog with a collar and chain. He started growling with the hair on his neck and back rising like a bristle brush. I started talking to the dog, but that didn't help. Using what nerve I possessed, I slowly reached toward the dog with the collar and chain. As quick as lightning, he slashed my hand and arm. I grabbed a snowshoe and gave him a dose of attitude adjustment. Again, I attempted to attach the collar and again he snarled and slashed at me. He had the largest fangs of any dog I had seen. I was thankful that the sled dogs normally slashed rather than bite. Those dogs possessed powerful jaws and I have seen them chew a large caribou bone into bits and pieces.

I finally attached the collar by holding a snowshoe in a threatening posture and using my free hand to attach the collar. I was shaking by the time I got the collar and chain on the dog. If a dog can sense fear, that dog knew I was scared. I decided to leave the harness on him. My hand and arm were bleeding from the slashing given me by the dog and I decided to leave well enough alone and let him sleep in his harness.

Later, I fed all the dogs their daily meal. The new dog sniffed at the food and wouldn't eat. To see a sled dog who wouldn't eat was really unusual. Normally the dogs never seemed to have enough to eat and would clean their food bowls completely. The new dog urinated on his food. After a few days he started eating like the rest of the dogs.

Until late May when the snow started to melt I would have to fight the Indian dog every time I hooked and unhooked him to the sled. Summer came and the dogs were chained along the shore of the river where I lived. Once a day I would tie three dogs to my belt and jog down the river beach for about one mile to give the dogs exercise.

My Headquarter's cabin was about three miles from the base. A Captain Fisher was the Communications Officer at the base. He was a former Naval Officer during World War II and after the war he transferred to the USAF. His wife and children were stationed with him on the base. He had heard about me so he and his family came down for a visit bringing an apple pie. I definitely welcomed them and the apple pie.

We became good friends and almost every Sunday he and his family would come down and spend most of the day with me. I would always have a stew made from wild game, onions and seasoned with salt and pepper. Some times the stew would be porcupine, rabbit or grouse. It seemed to always taste good when served with hot tea, fresh yeast rolls and strawberry jam. Often the Base Director of the Red Cross and the Base Chaplain would come down on a Saturday afternoon. We would play cards hour after hour. I really enjoyed their company.

Because of the dog team being tied in front of the cabin on the bank of the river, I was always careful to watch the Fishers' two small girls so that they wouldn't venture too near the dogs. One never knew what one of the dogs might do should they have the opportunity to grab one of the girls.

One day when they were visiting, we were busy into our card game when the dogs started howling. I almost panicked when I realized that the girls were no longer in the cabin. I envisioned the small girls being mauled severely by the dogs. I rushed outside and could hardly believe my eyes. The two small girls were playing with the "bad" Indian dog. One was on his back and the other was petting the dog while it licked her face. That incident broke the ice. After that the "bad" dog became one of my best dogs. He stopped attempting to bite me.

A few days after that incident, I attached that dog and two other dogs to my belt and we started the one-mile exercise run. We were almost at the end of our lap when a large porcupine leisurely strolled out of the woods in front of the dogs. The creature was probably heading to the river for a drink.

The dogs leaped forward pulling me off my feet and dragged me through the sand in an effort to reach the porcupine. I couldn't stop them before they reached the creature. Suddenly there was a yip and the dogs lost all interest in the porcupine.

They started whining and pawing at their faces. The porcupine had slapped each of the dogs and the Indian dog had taken a big bite out of the animal. His mouth gave the appearance of a beard from all the quills stuck into his face. I started the dogs running back to the cabin so that I could get pliers to remove the many quills stuck in their faces. I tied the dogs in their places and went to work.

Bud, the name I gave the new dog, had several quills stuck into the roof of his mouth. I removed the quills from the other two dogs first. Each of the dogs seemed to realize that I was helping ease their suffering. After I finished removing quills from the other two dogs, I, somewhat apprehensively, started on Bud.

I was wondering how it was going to work with me reaching inside his mouth with pliers to pull out the four or five large quills. It had to be done or the quills would work themselves deeper into his flesh and might even kill him. His large mouth and big fangs looked awesome.

I took a deep breath and reached part of my hand with pliers into his mouth. He whimpered a few times but made no effort to bite me. The dog realized he was being helped. After that he and I really bonded. Bud was a good sled dog and sad to say I lost him on an eight day hunting trip to the mountains. We got caught in a blizzard such that Labrador is infamous for and ran out of food. Bud pulled the sled until he had no strength left. Finally I tied him onto the sled as I worked across a thirty mile section of snow covered ice to a village where I could buy food and rest the dogs. The temperature was down to thirty below zero. He whimpered and chewed at the rope holding him to the sled and finally worked loose and attempted to regain his spot in the team. He didn't have the strength to keep up and the last I saw of Bud was his following the trail made by the sled. I didn't have the strength to help him because I was pulling the sled along with the dogs. The dogs and I were completely exhausted. I have always hoped that he made it to the village. I will never know because I had to return to the States the following week.

Parting with the dog team was very difficult. I was reassigned to Texas and even thought of taking my team with me. I didn't know it at that time, but that would have been impossible. After considerable thought I realized that I would be doing the dogs a big disservice by shipping them out of the Arctic to a warm area like Texas. Instead, I gave the team to my assistant in the Arctic Survival school. I

missed them, but realized that allowing the team to remain in the Arctic would be best for them. Memories of the dogs, the sled and cold climate will always be with me. Those were some of the best days of my life.

The Bad Dog

I once owned a large rusty brown dog that was a mixture of anyone's guess. He wasn't a bad looking dog and had shown up at our home in the country one spring day. He was very friendly with my four young children. I attempted to run him off, but each morning he would be back. I think my children had been slipping him food and he knew a good deal when he saw it. I then took an interest in him and started calling him "Rex" because I couldn't think of a good name for him.

Once we decided to adopt him, (It might have been the other way around), I connected a long wire between two trees and chained him with a long chain. He could still get his exercise and the children gave him a lot of petting and play. The reason I didn't allow him to run loose was because we lived near a road and Rex lived to chase vehicles. He would give chase about a quarter of a mile each time. I felt that it was only a matter of time before he was run over and killed.

Rex learned to slip his collar and get free. That was mostly at night because he was always back home by the time we were awake. The only way I could reinstall the collar was by bribing him with a can of dog food or table scraps. His neck was so thick that it was hard to keep a collar on him. He never attempted to bite when I reattached his collar.

Rex only lived with us for about four months. We never bonded as dog and master. He was very deceitful and did things when he thought no one was watching. At that time I was raising chickens (small scale for my family.) Once when we had to be away for most of a day I left him chained to his wire with plenty of shade, water and extra food.

When we returned late in the afternoon, Rex was lying in the shade, but his collar was off. He greeted us with a dog smile and much excitement. I noticed feathers and blood on his mouth. Oh no! I thought, I bet he has been after the chickens.

I rushed back to the small chicken house and found the door ajar. It was definitely closed and latched when we had left earlier in the morning. How the door got unlatched has always been a mystery.

In back of the chicken house chickens were sprawled all over the yard and some wedged into unbelievably small cracks. A few were dead, but most were playing "Chicken" or "dead." When I walked up to one of the chickens lying dead on the ground it raised its head and looked around and seeing me approach, quickly dropped its head and pretended to be dead.

The chickens wedged between the planks in the lumber pile were extracted and returned to the chicken house. Eventually, the rest of the chickens that had been playing dead suddenly came alive when I started feeding the other chickens and rushed for the chicken house door. To my surprise three or four chickens suddenly soared out the lower limbs of a tree where they had taken refuge.

Some dog lovers may not like how I disciplined Rex. I took one of the dead chickens and gave him some attitude adjustment by slapping him a few times with the chicken. I was angry, yet the whole incident was very humorous.

The next day a friend of mine who raised cattle about ten miles away was happy to receive a new pet dog. He had plenty of room for the dog to roam and roam Rex did. After only two or three days Rex roamed and never returned. I kept waiting for him to show up one day but he never did. I was relieved!

"Bud"

This story is about a dog that was the author's best friend and companion for six years. Bud was a Black Labrador Retriever who possessed the best characteristics of that breed of dog. He was intelligent, gentle and possessed traits of character that made him a family pet and friend. Yes, dogs can be a person's best friend!

Before Bud, the author had over the years owned several dogs including a small mixed breed white long-hair female dog. She was fun to watch. Her front legs were shorter than her rear legs. She was very intelligent, loyal and as good a protector of the family as a twenty-pound dog could be. She possessed character and displayed her good traits on a daily basis.

How we acquired Tricksie—we gave her that name because of the tricks she was always playing—is interesting because of the games she played with the SPCA whenever they attempted to capture her. She was abandoned near the SPCA shelter. At that time, we lived about a quarter of a mile from the shelter. She suddenly appeared in our yard one day and looked longingly at our door. I called the SPCA and they attempted to catch her. She always evaded their best efforts by hiding in the weeds near our yard. She

Bud

seemed to sense they were coming and once they came she would hunker down in the weeds and as soon as the "dog catchers" left she would suddenly appear outside our front door.

The representatives from the SPCA—once known as "Dog Catchers"—finally gave up their efforts and said they would occasionally stop by and attempt to nab the evasive little dog. They never caught her!

At first she was very timid and wouldn't approach when called. Perhaps she had been mistreated and didn't trust humans. At first we didn't want to do anything to attract her to our home. Maybe we were hoping she would go away. After a time we felt sorry for her and placed a bowl of water and some table scraps near the door for her. She cautiously approached the food, sniffed it and devoured everything in the bowl and drank most of the water. This went on for a few days. We started talking to the cute little dog until she would take food from our hands. She wore no collar, so there was no way we could discover to whom she belonged.

I decided to take her to the SPCA one day after she allowed me to pet her. She was so cute and laid down by my foot and looked up at me with the most serene look a dog could possess. After petting her the SPCA was no longer an option. We decided to keep her.

We led her into the house and she walked from room to room sniffing about everything in each room. She then walked over to a spot near the fireplace, gave a sigh of what seemed like contentment and took a long nap. She even rolled over once and gave a contented sigh. I think it wasn't just our family adopting her, she also adopted us.

Tricksie

Things didn't work too well at first. The second day that we allowed her in the house, we left her alone while we attended an evening church service. She didn't seem too pleased that we had left her home alone. When we returned, a surprise awaited us. We discovered just how displeased she was at being left home alone.

We drove into the carport and could hear Tricksie barking and scratching on the door. We were in for a shock when we unlocked the door and stepped into the house.

Apparently, Tricksie had panicked when we left her home. We couldn't believe the damage a small dog like Tricksie could do. The curtains hanging on the glass section of the door were shredded and on the floor. How in the world could such a small dog jump high enough to drag the curtains down? But she had. That was only a small part of the damage she did to our home. The trim around the door had been chewed and marred so badly that it had to be replaced. And to top that, she had shredded the carpet in front of the door, not only the front door, but the back door too.

She almost received a ride to the SPCA that very night. The thought came that maybe we could toss her over the fence at the Shelter and they would take care of her. We realized that after a certain period of time she would be put to sleep, so we didn't have the heart to proceed with our angry thoughts.

We did not like family pets to sit on chairs, beds or sofa. She apparently enjoyed a favorite rocking chair. Several times she was disciplined when we found her on the prohibited furniture. She was smart and maybe somewhat deceitful. She reached the point where she would never get on the banned furniture in our presence. However, one time we had left home and forgot something and returned to get that item. We entered the house and could see the rocking chair still rocking back and forth. She almost got caught in the act. She would never in our presence sit in that chair.

She lived indoors and would be allowed out in the evening before bedtime. She would remain outside for about thirty minutes, then would come to the door and bark indicating that she wanted back in.

One night she failed to return. She was called but failed to respond. Sometime later the doorbell rang and it was our neighbor bearing the bad news that "Tricksie" had been crossing the road and was struck by a car and killed instantly. That was such sad news! I buried her at the rear of the garage that same night. She was really missed.

Tricksie sometimes would cross the road when she was let out in the evening. Early one morning she wanted out. A few minutes later I heard the screech of car brakes and a crash. I rushed to the door and observed a car in the ditch near the road. I went over to offer help to the driver who was a young lady. The car had suffered severe damage. The woman called her husband and soon he arrived followed by a wrecker and the police. Luckily the woman wasn't hurt.

Her husband asked what caused her to brake so hard and skid into the ditch. She answered, "A cute little white dog was standing in the road and rather than hit it, I braked too hard and skidded into the ditch."

As she was telling her husband about the cause of the

accident, Tricksie walked over to where I was standing. Fortunately, neither the husband nor his wife noticed Tricksie. I quickly herded her behind the hedges and out of sight of those on the road where the accident occurred. It would have been embarrassing if she would have seen the dog and told her husband, "Look, there's the little dog that caused the accident."

We often reflect on how Tricksie was a joy to be part of our family. Her favorite thing was to lick each of our bare feet and especially our toes each evening. A wood stove at that time heated the house. She would lie down under the stove and seem to enjoy enduring the heat for a considerable time. Her thick mat of hair insulated her.

She was the first dog we had owned who wouldn't eat raw meat. If meat was cooked she would eat it. And she specially liked canned dog food. Her favorite food was table scraps. She was such a part of the family that she perhaps thought she should be eating at the table with us. No way!

She possessed a keen sense of hearing. Our family room was downstairs in a split-level home. We would be enjoying TV when she would suddenly jump up on the window ledge and start barking. Once this happened and apparently she had somehow detected a rabbit hopping through the yard. How she detected the rabbit we couldn't figure out. The same happened when anyone walked across the yard. Her senses were almost uncanny.

We were on vacation one year and Tricksie stayed home. A friend would stop by each day to play with her and give her the necessary food and water she needed. One night three boys broke into the house and attempted to locate whatever they could steal. After the police apprehended them, they confessed that a house they had broken into had a small white dog who kept after them until they became unnerved and hastily departed.

Another interesting incident that occurred involving this small dog was very humorous. We were cutting hay in a field adjacent to our yard. Occasionally a rabbit would dash in front of the tractor and to safety.

Tricksie loved being outside with me whenever I was working around the yard. This one particular time when we were cutting hay I observed the most interesting relationship between a wild Cotton Tail Rabbit and Tricksie.

The rabbit leaped in front of the tractor where it had been hiding in the tall grass and raced across the yard. Tricksie started chasing the rabbit and the two of them played chase for about thirty minutes. The rabbit would hide and the small dog would come charging up to where the rabbit was hidden and then they would chase each other. After a considerable time, they were both exhausted. They walked up and sniffed noses, stood there for several minutes sniffing each other, and then back to the chase.

When the mowing was completed there was Tricksie laying exhausted in the yard and there was no sign of the rabbit. How many dogs would become so friendly with a wild rabbit and the rabbit friendly toward a dog? The scene of the two sniffing noses would have made a beautiful picture. That goes to show how often when we need a camera it is packed away some place and difficult to retrieve at a moment's notice.

Perhaps the reader can feel the loss of such an interesting dog. Losing her was like losing a member of the family. After a time we decided to acquire another dog. That's when Bud comes into our life.

For a time Tricksie had a dog companion. This dog belonged to our daughter and her husband. He was a stray that had appeared at their door one day. He was brown with a small body. He reminded me of a grumpy old man. This dog was really different than Tricksie. They liked to play together and made good companions.

We kept this dog, named Boscoe, for a year while our daughter and husband lived out of state. That dog had a personality of his own. He was nothing but a grouch and was always growling at people.

The first night he stayed in our home was interesting. I had forgotten that the new dog was in the house. During the night, I placed my feet on the floor to get up for a trip to the bathroom. I was greeted suddenly by Boscoe growling at me from where he was sleeping under our bed. That scared me because I had forgotten that he was even in the house.

Matters became worse as I was returning from the bathroom. I walked by the dresser and there was Boscoe again growling at me. I kicked at him with my bare foot and he nipped my great toe. I was almost ready to toss that dog out into the night. Boscoe was a story in itself.

Boscoe was a very interesting dog. My daughter and son-in-law took him back to New Jersey with them. He was a good watchdog.

Boscoe

My daughter's husband worked at night and Boscoe made a good companion to her. One day she had worked hard all day and retired early. At about 1 AM, her husband returned from work. Boscoe would not let him enter the house. He was a snarling demon and scared him very much. He hammered on the door but my daughter was so deeply asleep that the hammering and the barking dog didn't awaken her. There was a phone in the bedroom next to the bed where his wife was sleeping so he drove around town until he located a payphone. He called her and after many rings, she sleepily answered the phone. She then unlocked the door and held Boscoe in her arms until her husband drove from the payphone back to their home. Needless to say, Boscoe's belligerent behavior toward him didn't make him grow very fond of that small dog.

Attempting to replace a departed and much loved dog can be very difficult. First, we didn't know what type of dog to get. Should we purchase a dog or acquire one from the Animal Shelter? We now lived on a twenty acre farm and decided that maybe we should get an outside dog that could serve as a good companion and watchdog.

It is sad that dogs are often abandoned and picked up by the SPCA. At that time they would only keep animals for a short time and if they weren't adopted they would be put to sleep. They didn't have the space to maintain a large number of animals. In some areas of the United States many dogs roam free and these wild dogs create a real problem.

When these so called "Wild Dogs" roam free they have been known to travel in packs, attack humans and kill farm animals. This is a growing problem all across the

USA. Wild cats are even a worse problem.

In order to save the life of a dog, we decided to adopt one from the Shelter. Selecting the right dog was important because we had young grandchildren who often visited our home. We didn't want a tempermental dog that we couldn't trust with children. We were thinking that adopting the right type of dog might be difficult.

Sometimes it is difficult to envision a dog's background, especially one that has been randomly picked up by the dog-catchers. One never knows the type of person who might have raised a dog. Dogs often take on the characteristics of their masters.

I will always remember when I walked into the "Death Row" part of the SPCA's animal shelter. Cells were filled with condemned dogs that would soon be put to asleep unless someone adopted them. This created a guilty feeling knowing that most of the dogs confined in these cells would be put to sleep. Maybe I could at least save one. I even thought of adopting more than one. That idea was quickly dropped. Sometimes having just one dog and giving it the proper care is sufficient for some people. That is evident when we see dogs being abused. Sometimes the abuse isn't physical but mental. Tying a dog up and never playing with it or properly caring for its needs is a type of abuse that is common with some dog owners.

Selecting the right dog might be more difficult than I originally thought. As I proceeded to walk through the hall with dogs locked in cells on each side, some barking, some growling, and some showing no interest in anything.

A big German Shepherd started growling on my approach. I decided that dog definitely wasn't for me. Then, there were yapping small dogs. There were hounds and some odd looking animals who appeared to have the worse characteristics of all the breeds that they inherited. In fact, they were ugly dogs!

One dog that really bothered me was a short-haired brown middle size dog who had retreated to the far corner of its cell where it lay showing no emotion at all. It had the weirdest eyes. They seemed to glow. That dog gave me a creepy feeling. I definitely didn't want a dog like that one.

The decision regarding which dog to select became easy when a large black Labrador Retriever came to its cell door as I approached and actually was wagging its tail like it was filled with joy that I was paying him attention. The Lab must have weighed seventy pounds. He was a nice size, black as the ace of spades, and one of the friendliest dogs I had ever seen.

He reared up on the wire gate with what looked like a smile on his face and seemed so happy to see me. I petted him and made the decision that he was the dog I wanted to adopt. It was love at first sight—I hoped on both sides.

In the office I told the attendant that I wanted the black Labrador Retriever. The lady smiled and remarked that the Lab was one of the best she could remember coming into the shelter. They were hoping someone would be interested in him so he wouldn't have to be put to sleep. He had been kept from the gas chamber several times, but now his time was up and he had to be put to sleep if he wasn't adopted. His name was Bud.

A family from Dover Air Force Base had owned him, and when they received orders for overseas, they had taken him to the shelter. He was a little over a year old. He was raised in a family of three children and received his name from lapping up Budweiser beer. He must have loved his beer! He was in for a disappointment because I don't drink beer. Having a dog named Bud brought back many memories from the past when I had another dog, named Bud. Perhaps those memories helped me decide on adopting this Bud.

The lady knew the family who had dropped Bud off at the shelter. Bud had been raised in a fenced in back yard in the Dover Air Force Base Housing. The three young children were always playing with Bud. He became very protective of the children and would never let strangers who were visiting get near the young children.

One time a large tomcat entered the fenced in yard and approached the children. When Bud sighted the large cat, he immediately grabbed the cat and tossed it across the yard. The astonished cat was over the fence in a split second to escape the enraged Labrador.

It had been a tough decision for the family to leave Bud who had become so much a part of their family. They had attempted to locate a family to take Bud, but none of their friends wanted a dog, and especially such a large dog.

I paid the necessary fees and was given papers for evidence of the shots he had been given. I had brought a collar and leash with me. He was a really happy dog. He walked and pulled with an eagerness that I remember from raising sled dogs many years before. He loved being made over, a characteristic that humans also enjoy.

Bud eagerly leaped into the front seat of the pickup. He seemed to be smiling and very happy. Once I reached home I showed Bud to my wife. She thought Bud was a bit large for her to handle, but she liked him anyway.

We decided that he would be an outside dog. I had a dog house located adjacent to our home where I chained him up during the day for a couple of weeks after we had acquired him. Every day I would take him for a walk around the property to acquaint him with things there. He started lifting his leg and marking various posts on the fence line. That was his territory and he wanted to insure other dogs understood that.

Once I let him loose and took him for a walk. He immediately started running toward a neighbor's home. I yelled for him to come back. He stopped, looked back and then willfully proceeded to continue his journey onto the other property. He ignored my command for him to come back onto our property. I raced to where he was, grabbed his collar and yanked him roughly back onto our property. I hit him a few times lightly with my hat. After that, he always obeyed my commands. The attitude adjustment I rendered him really had a positive affect on his behavior without doing any physical harm.

It wasn't long until he was allowed to roam around the property. I acquired a small rubber ball and Bud and I would play for twenty or so minutes each day. I would toss the ball and he would retrieve it and bring it to me. He would drop the ball at my feet and wait impatiently for me to toss the ball again. I could tell when he was tired playing ball with me. He would grab the ball and go lay down and refuse to get up. That was like him saying, "enough is enough."

In bad weather he would sleep in the garage and a number of times when the temperature would drop to the low teens, I would allow him to sleep in the heated hallway that ran from the garage to the house. He always seemed to be uncomfortable in the house and could hardly wait to be let out.

After he was allowed to run loose on the property, he became a fantastic watch dog. In the summer he would sleep on the deck by the sliding glass door to our bedroom. We would leave the main door open and enjoy the breeze coming in through the screen door. Bud would sleep next to the door and several times each night he would get up and walk around the entire house and come back and lay down. Eventually, he wore a path around the house. We felt very secure having him for a watchdog.

We had a seven-hundred-foot drive leading from the main road to our home. Anytime someone drove up our lane, or even turned into the lane, Bud would let us know we had company. On occasion he wouldn't allow people to get out of their vehicles. He would be snarling with the hair standing up on his back. He didn't like people with beards and long hair, plus he didn't like people of another race. He was strange about that. Many times when a vehicle would drive up to our home, Bud would take a dislike for the occupants. He seemed to especially dislike pickups. I would have to put him in the garage, and once he was locked up, he became quiet.

He was really good with children. When he was eating they could get on his back, and if they dared, take his food from him. Sometime he would give a warning growl, but he never attempted to bite any of them. The only time I saw him get upset with children was when my grandchildren brought a cute little girl of another race over to see Bud. She came too close and Bud actually snapped at her. I believe he was warning her to stay away from his food dish.

Bud's action upset me, and of course the little girl was very scared from the ordeal. After all, having a large dog lunge at you and snapping in your face would be unnerving for anyone regardless of age. After that incident, I told the grandchildren not to play with Bud when he was eating and especially, not to bring company into where he was eating.

We took him to a dog grooming business on a regular schedule to have him dipped for fleas and ticks. He disliked me leaving him, but he behaved well and the person working with him became very fond of him. A large bandana was always tied around his neck when he went for grooming. He really got to like having that around his neck.

He was always really happy to see me when I would go to pick him up. Perhaps he was afraid of being abandoned like his original family had done to him. He would be leaping for joy and would attempt to jump up on me. That was taboo and I would bring my knee up to repel him back. He would get the message that leaping on me was unacceptable behavior and would immediately stop.

As the years flowed past we learned to appreciate that Bud was such a wonderful dog. I couldn't imagine a dog being any better than him. When he was really happy he would have a big smile on his face. People may think dogs don't smile, but I'm sure they do when they are happy.

One really hot day I missed Bud and wondered where he was. I called and he didn't come. I started looking for him and everywhere I looked, no Bud. I was becoming concerned, and as I was walking by one of our ponds, I happened to glance down into the pond and there was Bud submerged in the pond with only his nose and eyes above the surface of the water. He was in thick cattails and difficult to see. He remained there for several hours and only came out late in the afternoon. Often during hot weather I would attempt to spray him with the water hose. He was scared to death of being sprayed and would rush off and hide.

One of our neighbors really took a liking to Bud and Bud to him. The neighbor often had company and cooked prime ribs on the grill. Bud would sneak over and patiently wait some distance away for my neighbor and his guests to complete their meal. Once my neighbor finished eating, he would give Bud a rib to chew on.

I knew that the neighbor wanted Bud to stop by and see him so I didn't mind. Several times during the summer months Bud would go visiting just when the neighbor was cooking prime ribs. I guess his keen sense of smell detected that food was being grilled. He would return with a bone in his mouth and a bag of rib bones tied to his neck. He would walk over to me and I would take the bag loose from his neck and he would lie down and chew on his bone. I would, during the next few days, give him one of the bones to gnaw on.

One day we finished eating a watermelon and a cantaloupe and placed the rinds in a trashcan in the garage. A short time later Bud suddenly leaped to his feet from where I was petting him and raced for the garage. I thought that maybe he had spotted a cat entering the garage. Cats weren't on of his list of favorite animals. I followed and noticed the trashcan turned over and a large groundhog eating on the rinds.

Bud didn't know what to make of the strange critter who had invaded his space. He walked cautiously toward the groundhog. He stretched his neck out and started to sniff the groundhog. That animal didn't want to have anything to do with such a large creature as Bud.

As Bud sniffed, the groundhog bit Bud on the nose. That was disaster for the groundhog. Bud went berserk when the groundhog bit his nose. It was just like a person losing his temper. Moving like a streak of lightening, Bud grabbed the unfortunate animal by the neck and tossed it about twelve feet. He then rushed over and grabbed it by the neck again and shook it back and forth until it was dead. It all happened in a flash.

There was a small colony of groundhogs living in the orchard where they had dug some den holes. During the next few days Bud went on a rampage killing groundhogs. I walked through the orchard several days later and discovered three groundhogs dead in the orchard. After that we had no more groundhog problems. Bud had solved that problem.

Before that incident groundhogs had never been a concern of mine. Several years before when my land was in pasture, I raised a few head of cattle and the ground was covered with ankle deep clover.

One very dry year the water had dried from the back ditch. Late one afternoon I saw movement in the clover. It was a mother groundhog walking across the field toward my pond. Behind her trailed five small groundhogs in a single row following in a straight line. That was the cutest sight! I didn't disturb them and watched as they all lined up on the edge of the pond and drank for a short time. The mother groundhog returned the way she had come with the half-grown family following her. That was another time I wished I had a camera handy. If I would have had Bud at that time the ground-hogs would have been in peril.

Any other dog who dared to enter Bud's domain immediately was apprehended, sniffed and then the chase would start. Bud would chase the other dogs until they crossed the property line. Then he would proudly return to the house. He always returned to the house where he acted like he should be congratulated on a job well done. It didn't take me long to realize that he loved praise. I would pet him and tell him what a good dog he was. Often I would give him a treat. Both dogs and people love praise for their actions.

Labrador Retrievers are a breed of dogs made for work. The black Labrador first came to notice in southeastern Labrador. Thus the name Labrador came about. The Labrador quickly became popular in neighboring Canada and the United States.

This breed is made for work. Newfoundland fishermen started using this breed to work in the cold surf to help pull in nets that were set for codfish. The lab's fur is short and dense, with its back and tail resembling an Otter. It is well adapted for working in or near cold water.

Over the ensuing years, the Labrador has achieved worldwide fame as a great and gentle retriever and family dog.

Bud had never experienced hunting. He would see flocks of ducks and geese flying over and would become excited. Perhaps a basic instinct was aroused whenever waterfowl would fly over.

We had three small ponds on our property. The ponds were stocked with fish and that soon attracted Blue Herons. The Herons are great fishers armed with a long spear like beak. After a time, several herons would visit our ponds on a regular basis and spear many fish. The only problem was that many of the catfish were too large for the Herons to swallow.

They would kill a fish, attempt to swallow it, and when that failed it would drop the fish and go spear another. It was fun to watch their frustration at not being able to swallow the big catfish. They would go through all kinds of gyrations in an attempt to down the fish. They were about to clean out our ponds.

One day I discovered six nice size catfish dead on the bank of the pond. Each had a neat hole in its head from being speared by a Heron. When Bud came to live with us, he immediately took a dislike for Herons. He spent a lot of time attempting to ambush them. I don't know if he ever caught one or not, but he would follow snapping at the feet of a Heron as it attempted to get airborne. His dislike for Herons saved a lot of fish. We would be sitting on the deck during the cool of the evening when Bud would suddenly rush from the deck toward one of the ponds. Next we would see Bud running and leaping into the air in an effort to nab a Heron that he had just scared from the pond.

One damp winter day Bud went missing. I remembered that he had followed me to the back of the property and I didn't remember him returning with me. Later in the afternoon when he still hadn't returned I became concerned. By then he was like a family member.

It was winter and the ground was wet. I walked back to where he had been with me earlier and started tracking him. It seemed like he stopped to sniff every brush pile or clump of grass. Then his tracks headed in a beeline straight across the neighbor's field toward where several goose pits were located. Each pit was about five feet deep with a removable lid. One was open and there was Bud in the bottom. The walls and bench of the pit were scratched from Bud's effort to escape from the pit. I had never seen a dog so happy as Bud was to see me. After I got him out, he walked close to me all the way home.

When dove season started I was excited that Bud would have the opportunity to retrieve any doves that I might drop. The edge of the field where we were hunting was next to a soybean field. The beanstalks were about two feet high with lots of foliage. After a time the dove started flying and the shooting started. Bud didn't know what to make of all the noise. He pressed his body tightly against my leg for protection and after a short time relaxed.

Finally I dropped a dove and sent Bud into the soybean field to retrieve the bird. He raced to where the bird had fallen and after a moment of sniffing found the bird and brought it to me. That was a wonderful moment for Bud and me. I was proud and he looked proud of himself. This went on for two hours and I dropped several more doves which Bud retrieved.

I noticed that Bud was sneezing and discovered that the small dove feathers were sticking inside his mouth. I spent some time attempting to get all the small feathers out of his mouth. Later I read that Labs have so much moisture in their mouths that they shouldn't be used to retrieve dove and other small birds.

We started traveling for business purposes each winter for two to three months at a time. We left Bud home because it would have been too difficult taking him with us. Our daughter and son-in-law would stop by and lock him in the garage at night, feed and water him, and sometimes pet and make over him. Still, he seemed to miss us when we were away and would be very excited when we came home.

He expressed his joy by racing around the house at full speed several times and rubbing against my leg. He didn't want to be out of our sight for a few days after we returned. Of course, he received lots of attention once we were home. While we were away, he always put on weight. I guess he was being fed too much and not getting the proper exercise.

When we returned from a three-month trip at Christmas one year, we were surprised that Bud didn't do his usual joyful antics on seeing us. He just stood around until I went over and petted him. He had no energy, but he seemed very happy to see us. He came over to where I was sitting and placed his head on my knee and looked up with those beautiful ebony eyes like he adored the ground I walked on. I gave him lots of attention for a few days, but he wasn't the same Bud as he once was. He looked like he had gained a lot of weight, didn't run anymore and I soon discovered that he didn't have the energy to walk up the steps into the house much less getting into the pickup.

I called our veterinarian and arranged for an appointment for Bud. A few days later I took Bud to the vet. He was so weak that I had to lift him into the cab of the pickup. All kinds of tests were made on Bud. The results of the tests were that Bud had advanced congestive heart failure. He could be given pills each day, but would never regain the energy he once had. I was told that his condition would deteriorate, even with the medicine, until he wouldn't be able to walk. The veterinarian recommended that Bud be put to sleep.

That came as a shock to me. I thought his problem could be fixed with medicine. Bud had gained to 112 pounds while we were away. That was much too heavy. Humans and dogs have this same trait. Gaining weight and not getting exercise results in all types of medical problems. Sadly, I agreed that my beloved Bud would be put to sleep. I couldn't stand the thought of him suffering further. He rested his head on my knee and looked up at me with those large sad looking ebony eyes until he closed them and fell asleep. I held him for a time and could hardly control my sorrow. He had been one of the finest dogs that we ever had. I believe he adopted us the same as we adopted him. There has to be a heaven for good dogs like Bud. He will always be in my thoughts.

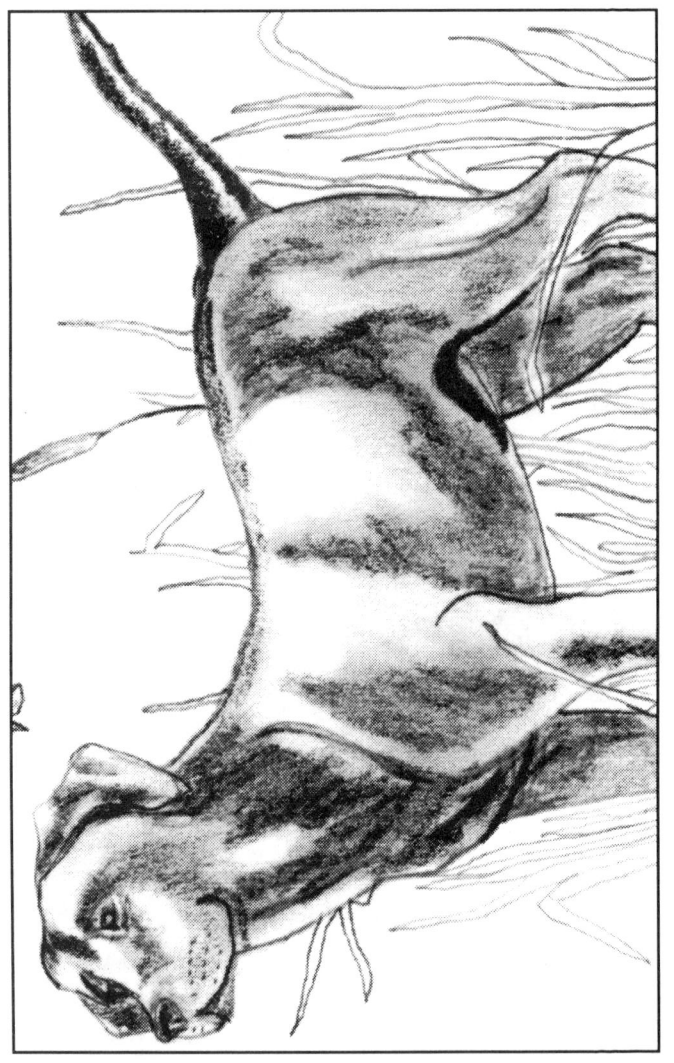
Bud

The Red Dog
by
Gladys Brown

The red dog appeared on a Sunday Morning in November at River Ridge, our home in Connecticut. She was there when we left for church and had come to greet us from the direction of the compost heap.

She appeared to be part Spaniel, and some unknown breed, but she was definitely dusty-red. She had recently had, or was about to have pups, and we decided she must belong to someone and probably would be gone when we got back from church. But she was not gone.

Our daughter kept going out to her and finally took her for a long walk down the lane, without a leash hoping that someone would come out and see her, or she would recognize a familiar landmark and find her way home. But she trotted back to our place behind our daughter and went back to the compost heap and lay down.

Night came with a light wind and rain, and a radio forecast of possible sleet or snow. "I just can't stand the thought of her being out there hungry and cold while our animals are well-fed and warm." I said. So my daughter went to where she was bedded down on the compost heap, fed her an evening meal and put her in the garage. We gave her two old blankets that she accepted with dignity, lying down on them as we went out the door.

All the next day she hung around. The sun was out, and the rain and wind were gone. The sleet and rain had not happened. She took another walk with my daughter, again without a leash and in another direction from the day before. Again, she followed my daughter home.

The mailman stopped by and when we asked him if he knew who owned her. He looked her over and said, "I never saw her before around here. Maybe she wandered here from over in New York State." We ruled that out because of the distance, and then he suggested we try the new people on the horse farm a half mile away. No luck there!

About ten on Election Day two fellows showed up "to fence in the back forty," They said. Actually it was only 500 feet of fencing across the back of the home place to keep our two Scottish Terriers within bounds.

When they saw her, one of them looked at her and said, "If she is still here at the end of the day, I'll take her. I have four children under five years old, and if they don't get too rough with her, I'll keep her. But first I'll take her to the vet and see if she's okay."

By then we had advertised over the local radio station with no results. We all decided that the Dog Warden would only put her to sleep without even trying to find her owners.

She stayed on the compost heap where she could bed down in the grass close by. The sun was warm, and with the heat generated by the compost, she seemed quite comfortable, rising only to gratefully accept food from the fence men's lunches.

The workday came to an end for the fence men about three-thirty.

"Here girl," said the dark, slim man with the four children.

They drove away with "girl" on the younger man's lap. She appeared to be happy and friendly toward them. We wished her well and went into the house.

We wondered why she picked our place to stay, back from the road, and on the river's edge. At least she had two days of safety, some food, and a little love, and the promise of more to come.

We found out later that she was an older lady, but was definitely going to have pups, and soon. She had gone out in the chill of November risking the cold, and knowing hunger, to find a home and safely for her coming family? She was just a mixed-breed red dog, but she had a mother's heart.